PIANO | VOCAL | GUITAR • AUDIO   **VOLUME 62**

PIANO PLAY-ALONG

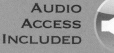

AUDIO
ACCESS
INCLUDED

BILLY JOEL
HITS

PLAYBACK+
Speed • Pitch • Balance • Loop

To access audio visit:
www.halleonard.com/mylibrary

Enter Code
2661-0977-3836-6835

Cover photo © Nancie Hemminger/Ebet Roberts

ISBN 978-1-4234-4961-4

HAL•LEONARD®

7777 W. BLUEMOUND RD. P.O. BOX 13819 MILWAUKEE, WI 53213

In Australia Contact:
Hal Leonard Australia Pty. Ltd.
4 Lentara Court
Cheltenham, Victoria, 3192 Australia
Email: ausadmin@halleonard.com.au

Visit Hal Leonard Online at
www.halleonard.com

PAGE TITLE

THE ENTERTAINER

Words and Music by
BILLY JOEL

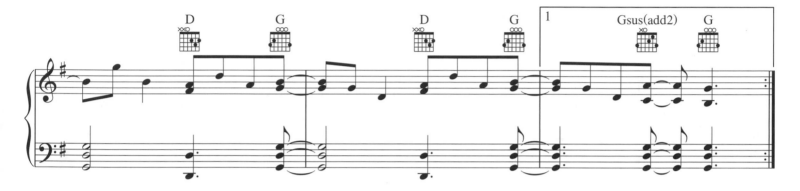

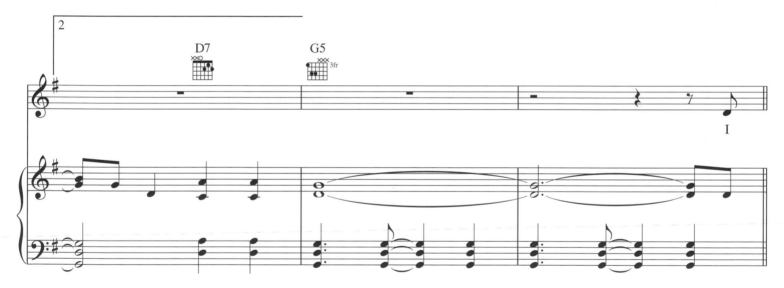

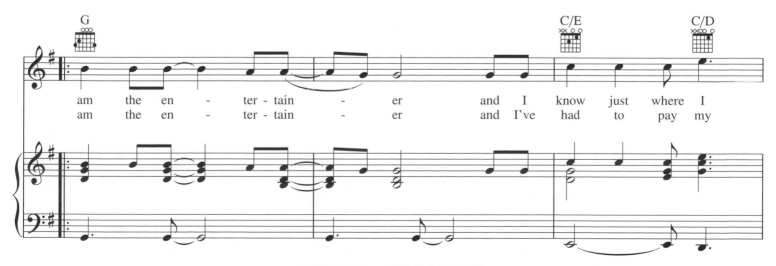

am the en- ter-tain- er and I know just where I
am the en- ter-tain- er and I've had to pay my

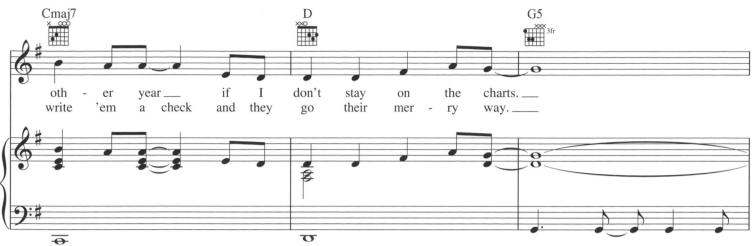

oth - er year ___ if I don't stay on the charts. ___
write 'em a check and they go their mer - ry way. ___

am the en - ter - tain - er, ___ been all a - round ___ the world. ___
am the en - ter - tain - er; ___ I bring to you ___ my ___ songs. ___
am the en - ter - tain - er; ___ I've come to do ___ my ___ show. ___
am the en - ter - tain - er, ___ the i - dol of ___ my ___ age. ___

___ I played all kinds of pal - ac - es and
___ I'd like to spend a day ___ or two;
___ You heard my lat - est rec - ord, ___ it's
___ I make all kinds of mon - ey ___ when

C   D   G

laid all kinds of girls. ____ I can't re-mem - ber fac -
I can't stay that long. ____ I got to meet __ ex - pens -
been on the ra - di - o. ____ It took me years __ to write
I go on the stage. ____ You see me in ____ the pa -

C/E   Dm7   C

- es, I don't re - mem - ber names, __ oh, but
- es, I got to stay in line. ____ Got - ta
____ it; they were the best years of my life. ____ It was a
- pers; I've been in the mag - a - zines. ____ But if

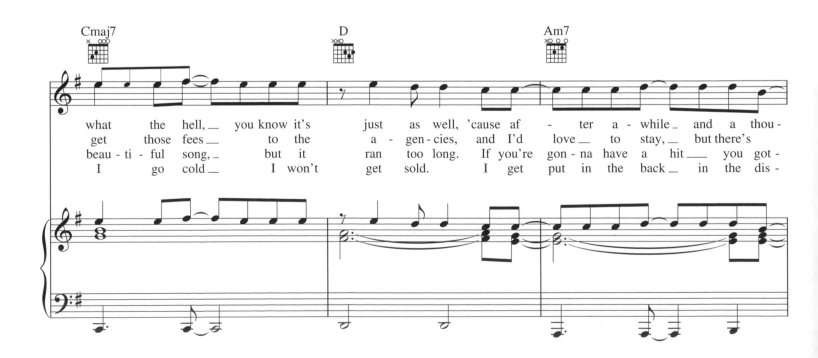

Cmaj7   D   Am7

what the hell, __ you know it's just as well, 'cause af - ter a - while __ and a thou -
get those fees __ to the a - gen - cies, and I'd love __ to stay, __ but there's
beau - ti - ful song, __ but it ran too long. If you're gon - na have a hit __ you got -
I go cold __ I won't get sold. I get put in the back __ in the dis -

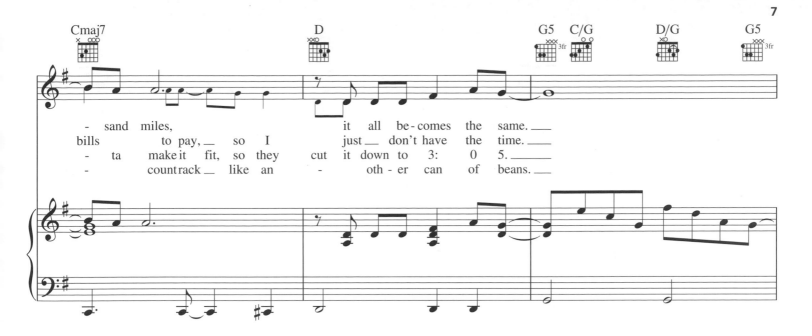

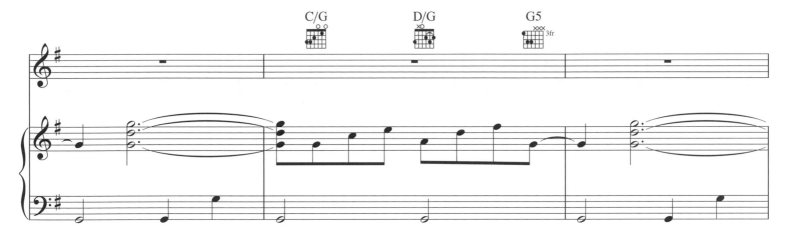

C/E G7/D C

-er and I know just where I stand: An-

G/B C

-oth - er ser - e - nad - er and an - oth - er long - haired band.

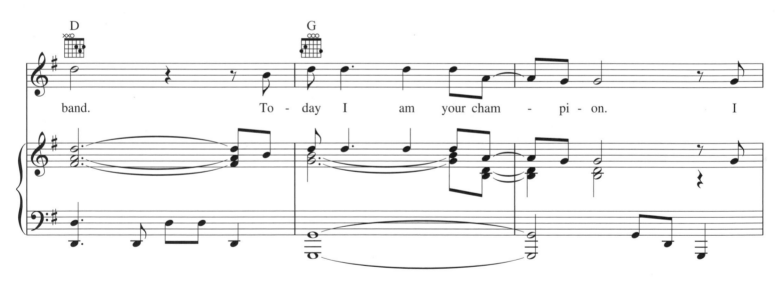

D G

band. To - day I am your cham - pi - on. I

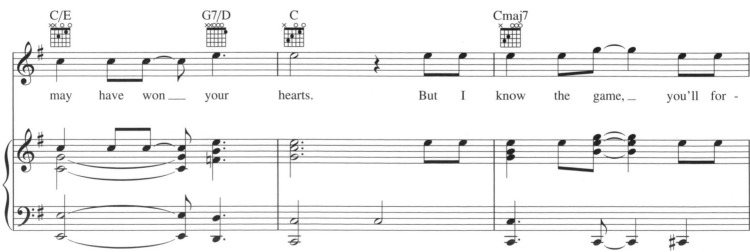

C/E G7/D C Cmaj7

may have won ___ your hearts. But I know the game, ___ you'll for-

get my name. ___ I won't be here in an - oth - er year ___ if I

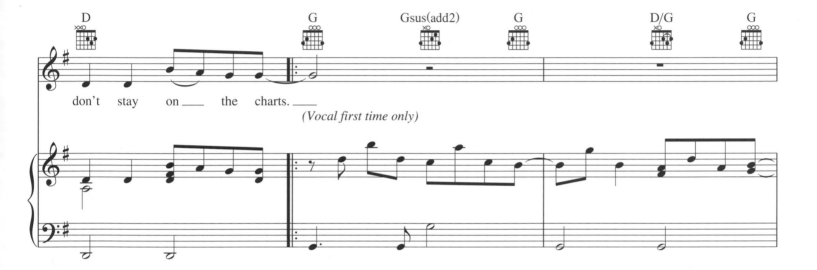

don't stay on ___ the charts. ___

(Vocal first time only)

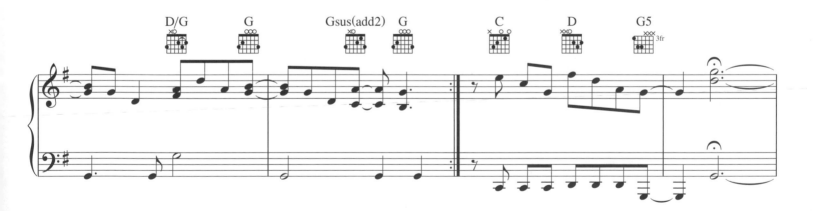

HONESTY

Words and Music by
BILLY JOEL

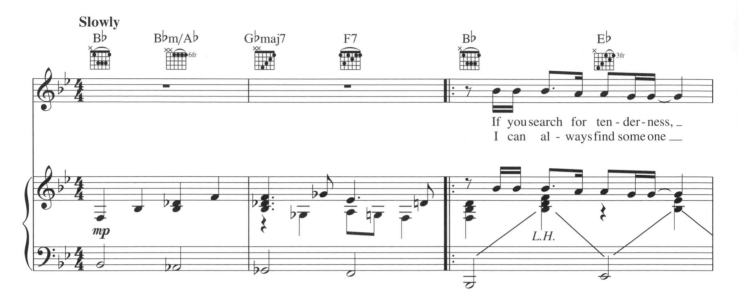

Slowly

If you search for ten-der-ness,
I can al-ways find some one

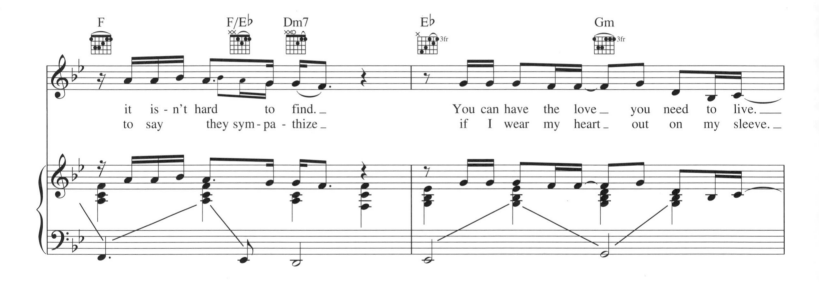

it is-n't hard to find. ___ You can have the love ___ you need to live. ___
to say they sym-pa-thize ___ if I wear my heart ___ out on my sleeve. ___

And if you look for truth - ful - ness ___ you might
But I don't want some pret - ty face ___ to

just as well — be blind; — it al-ways seems to be — so hard — to give. —
tell me pret - ty lies. — All I want is some - one to — be - lieve. —

Hon - es-ty — is such a lone - ly word. —

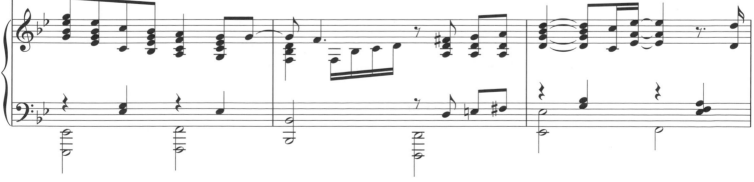

Ev-'ry-one is so un - true. — Hon - es-ty — is

To Coda ⊕

hard-ly ev - er heard, _____ but most-ly what I need from you. ___

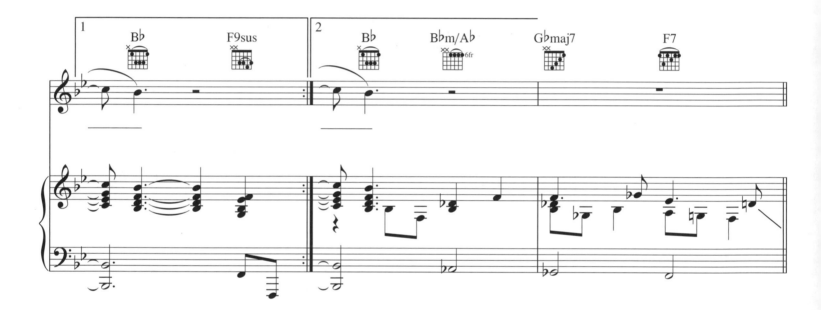

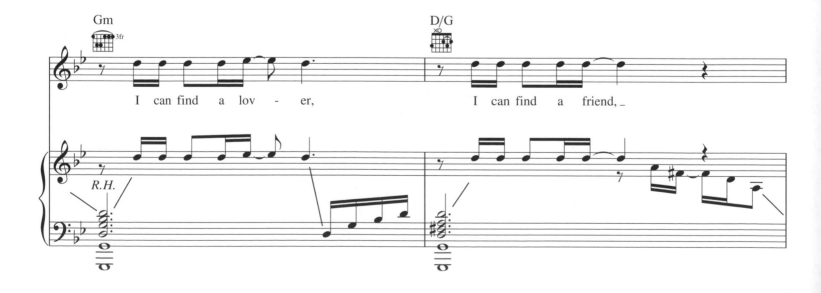

I can find a lov - er, I can find a friend, _

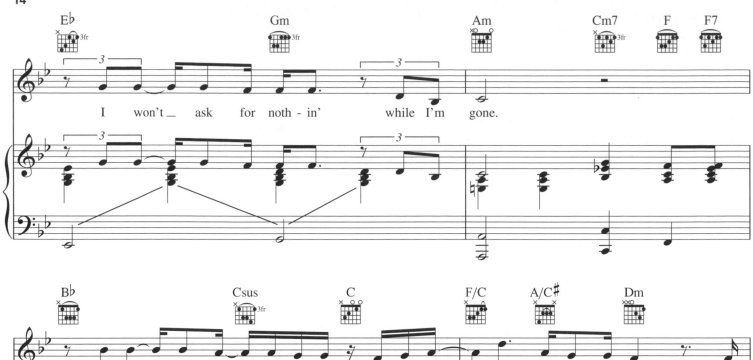

I won't ___ ask for noth-in' while I'm gone.

When I ___ want sin-cer-i-ty, tell me, where ___ else can I turn? ___ 'Cause

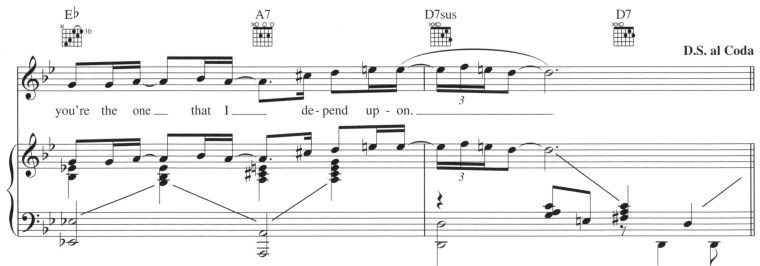

D.S. al Coda

you're the one ___ that I ___ de-pend up-on. ___

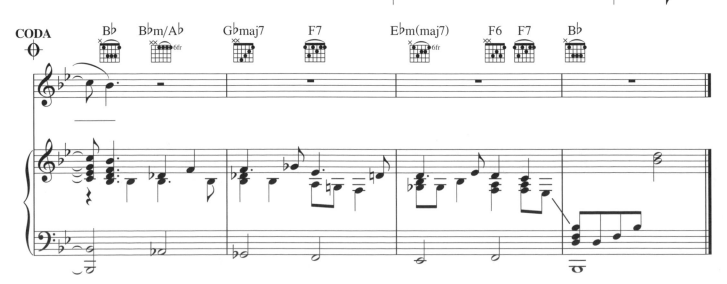

CODA

JUST THE WAY YOU ARE

Words and Music by
BILLY JOEL

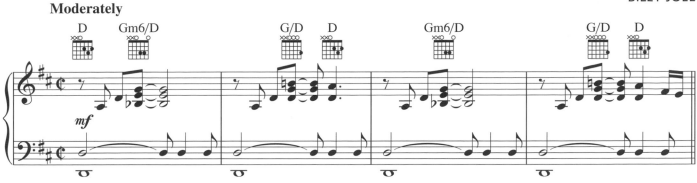

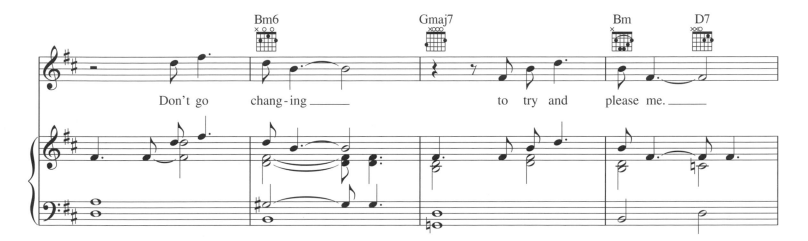

Don't go chang-ing ___ to try and please me. ___

You nev-er let me down _ be-fore. ___ Mm, ___ mm. ___

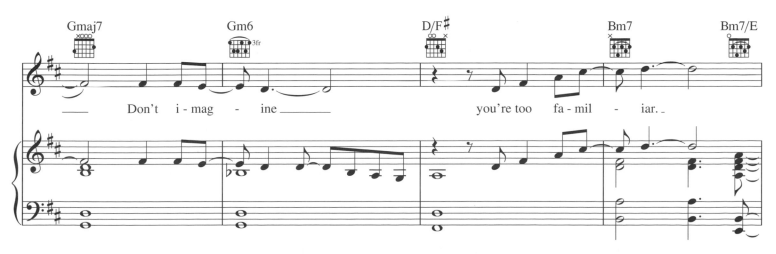

___ Don't i-mag - ine ___ you're too fa-mil - iar. ___

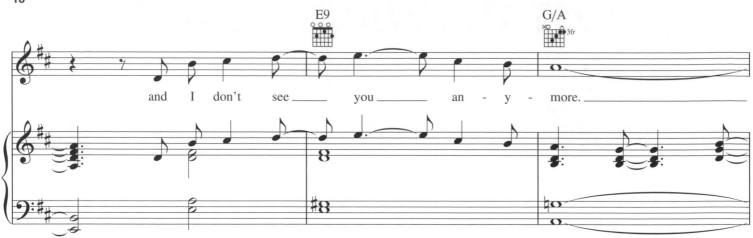

and I don't see____ you____ an - y - more._____

____ I_____ would__ not leave you_____ in times of

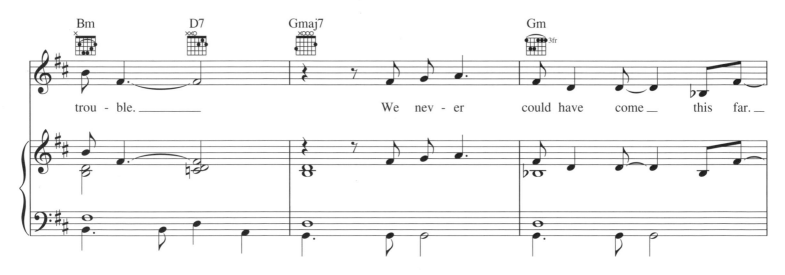

trou - ble._____ We nev - er could have come__ this far.

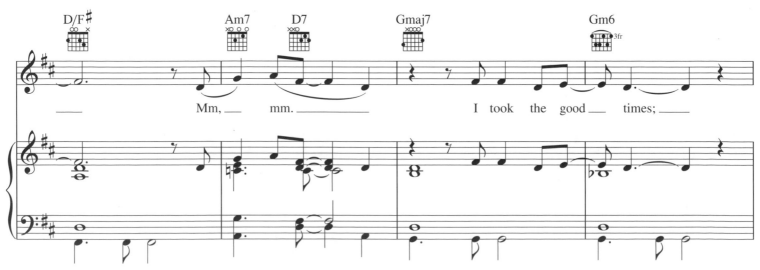

____ Mm,____ mm._____ I took the good__ times;____

I'll take the bad ____ times. _____ I'll take you just ____

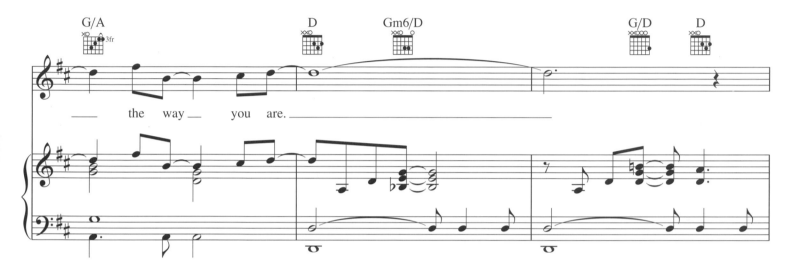

____ the way ____ you are. _____

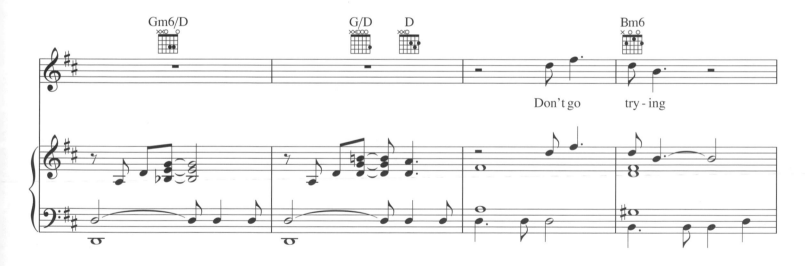

Don't go try - ing

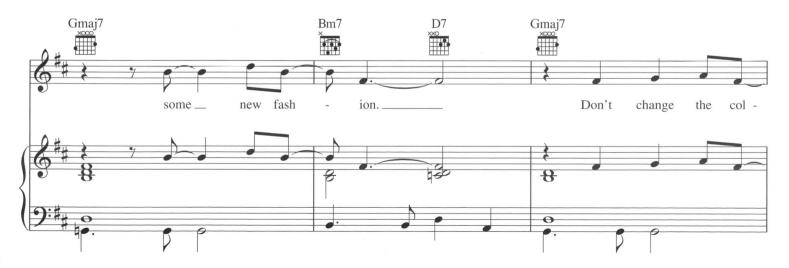

some ____ new fash - ion. _____ Don't change the col -

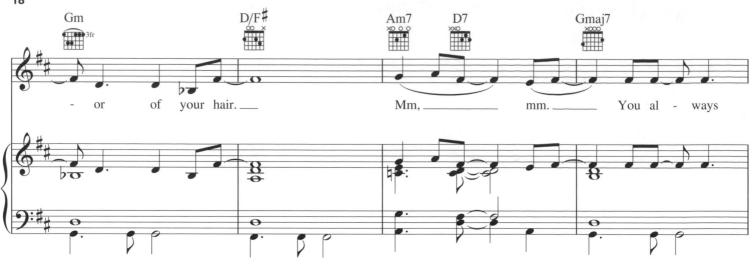

- or of your hair. ___ Mm, _____ mm. ___ You al - ways

have my un - spo - ken pas - sion, ___

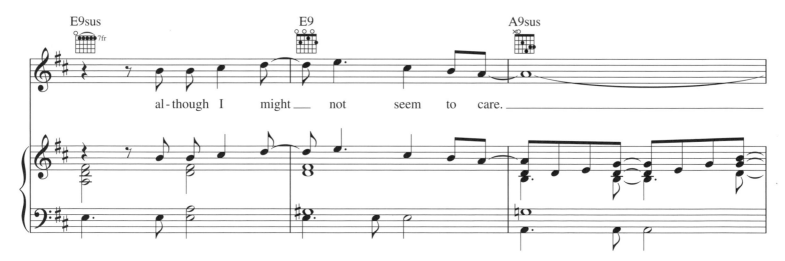

al - though I might ___ not seem to care. ___

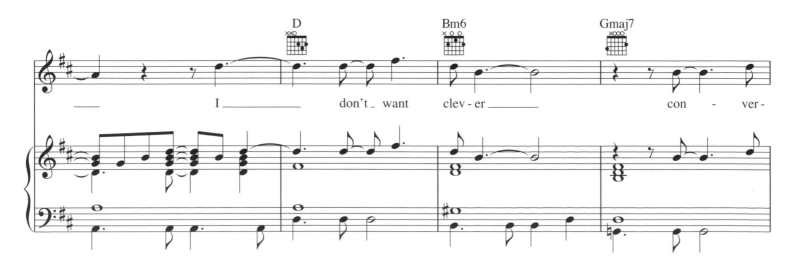

___ I _____ don't _ want clev - er _____ con - ver -

sa - tion; _____ I nev - er want to work _ that hard. _

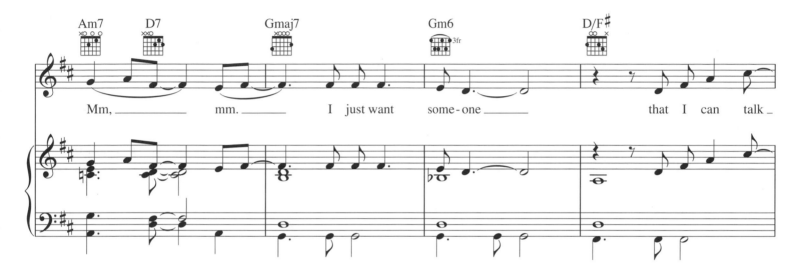

Mm, _____ mm. _____ I just want some - one _____ that I can talk _

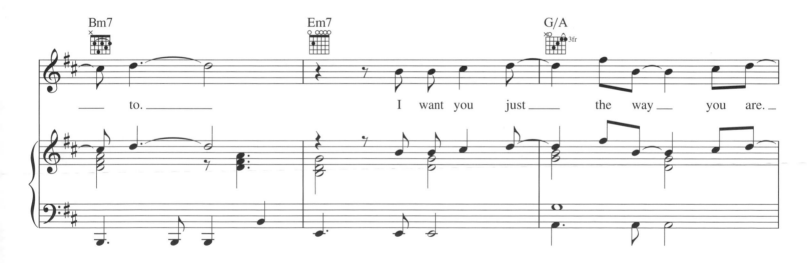

_____ to. _____ I want you just ____ the way _ you are. _

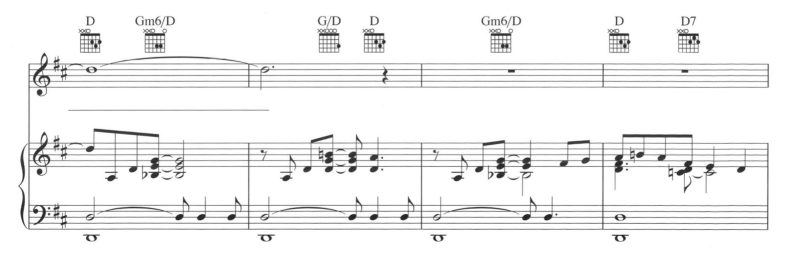

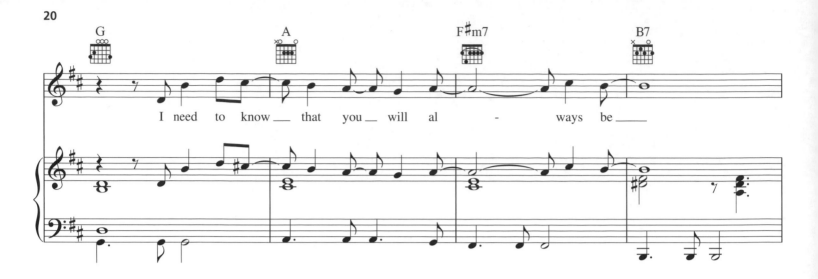

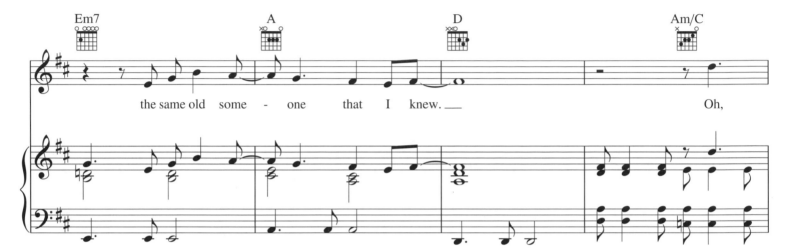

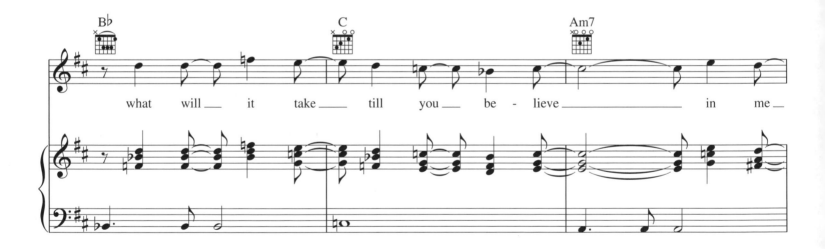

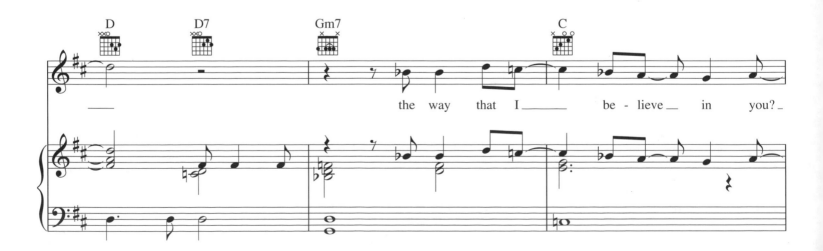

I _____ said ___ I love you, _____
(D.S.) *Instrumental solo*

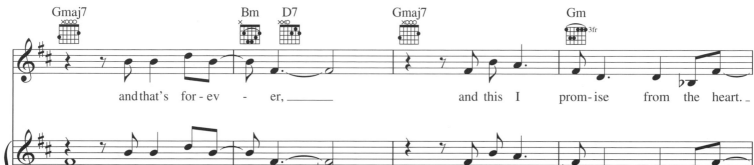

and that's for - ev - er, _____ and this I prom - ise from the heart. _

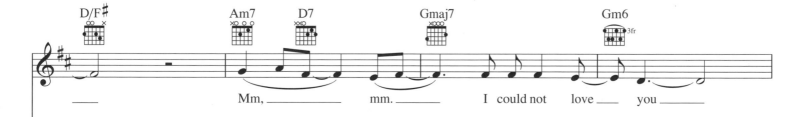

___ Mm, _____ mm. _____ I could not love ___ you _____

To Coda

an - y ___ bet - ter. _____ I love you just _

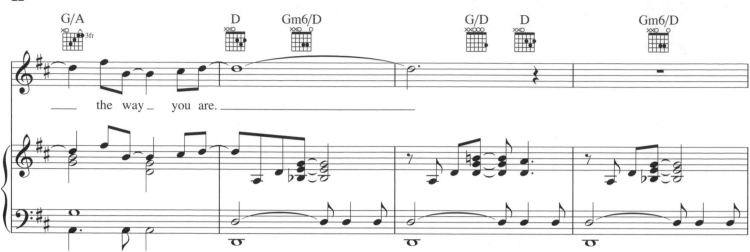

the way ___ you are. _____

D.S. al Coda

CODA

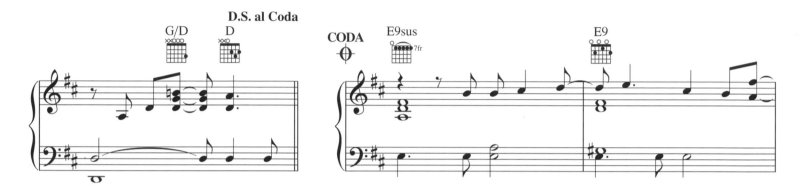

Solo ends I _____ don't ___ want clev - er _____

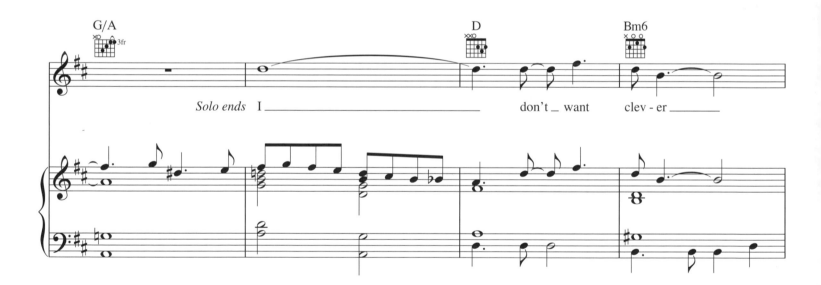

con - ver - sa - tion; I nev - er

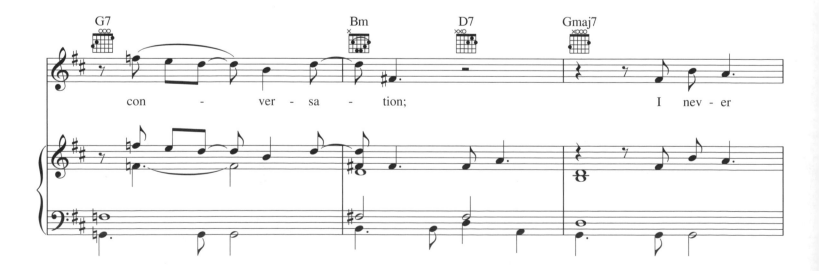

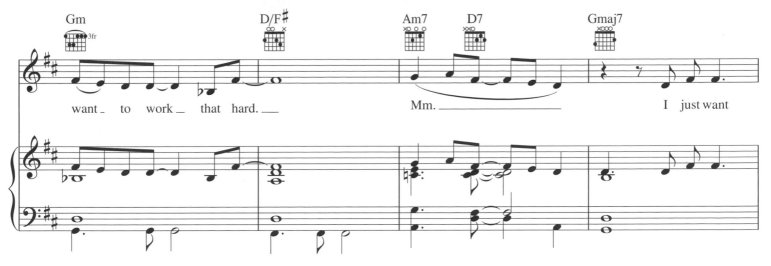

want to work that hard. Mm. I just want

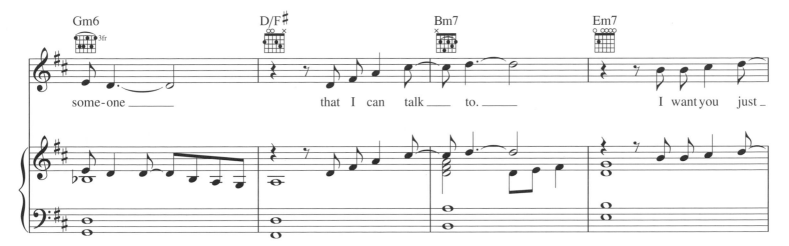

some-one that I can talk to. I want you just

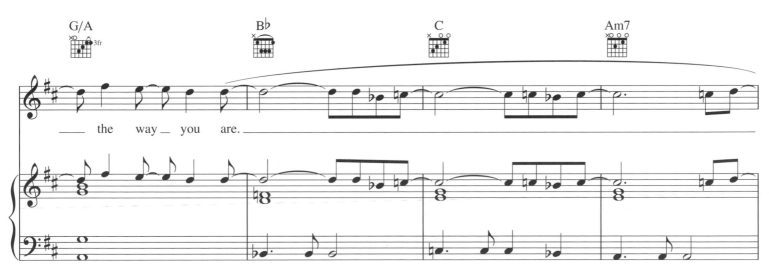

the way you are.

Whoa.

THE LONGEST TIME

Words and Music by
BILLY JOEL

Bright Rock and Roll

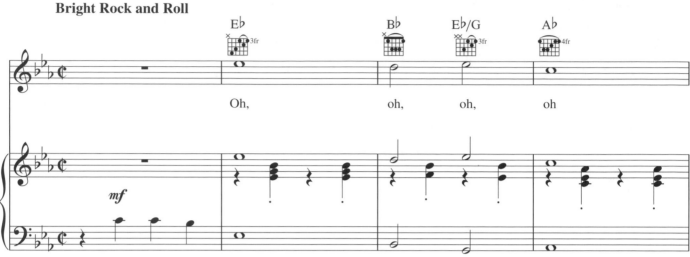

Oh,   oh,   oh,   oh

L.H. played an octave lower throughout

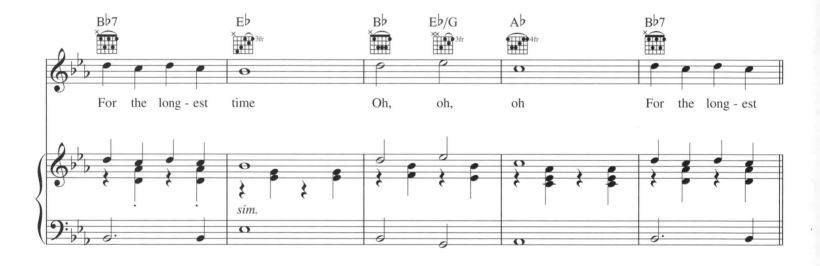

For the long-est time   Oh,   oh,   oh   For the long-est

sim.

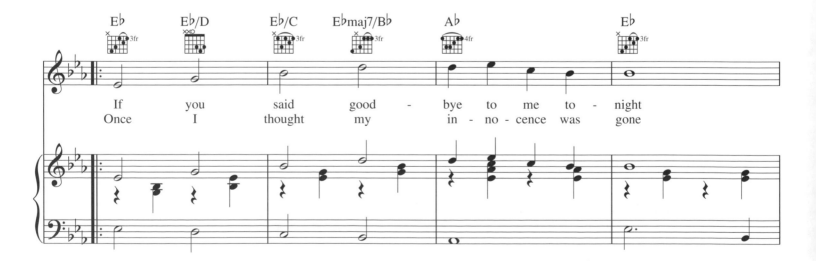

If   you   said   good - bye to me to-night
Once   I   thought   my   in - no - cence was   gone

There would still be mu-sic left to write
Now I know that hap-pi-ness goes on

What else could I do
That's where you found me

I'm so in-spired __ by you
When you put your arms a-round me

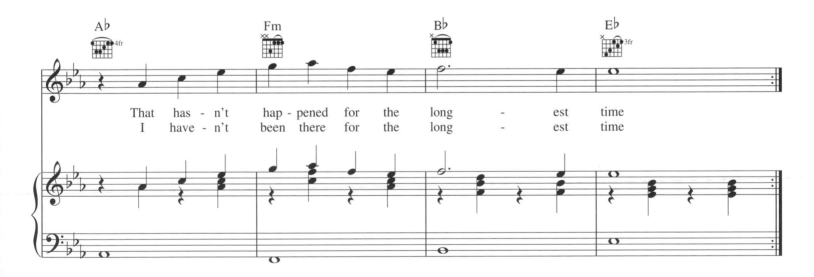

That has-n't hap-pened for the long - est time
I have-n't been there for the long - est time

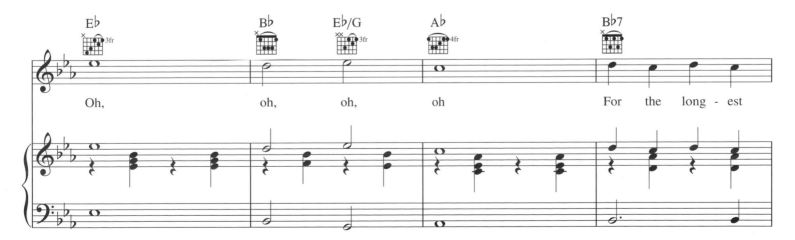

Oh, oh, oh, oh For the long - est

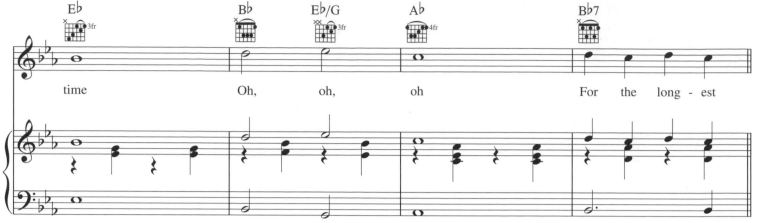

time   Oh,   oh,   oh   For the long - est

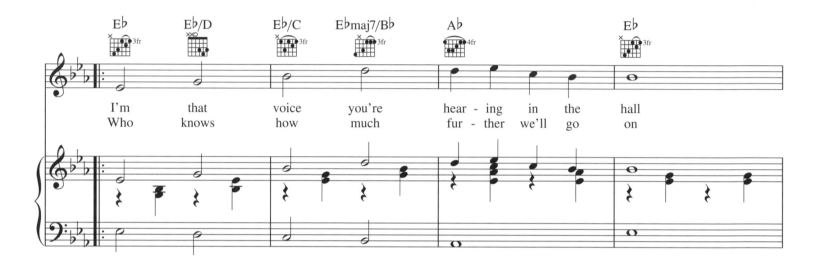

I'm   that   voice   you're   hear - ing   in the   hall
Who   knows   how   much   fur - ther   we'll   go   on

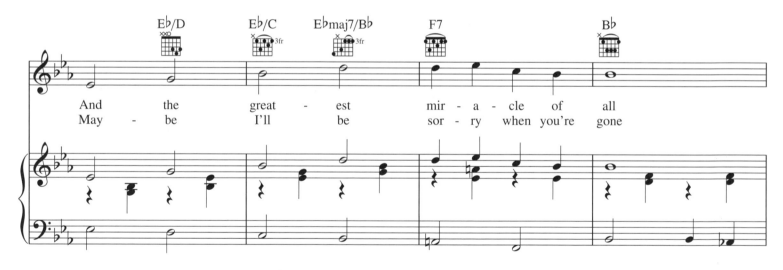

And   the   great - est   mir - a - cle   of   all
May - be   I'll   be   sor - ry   when you're   gone

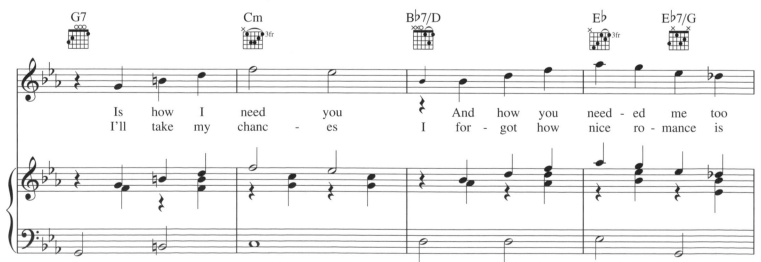

Is   how   I   need   you   And   how   you   need - ed   me   too
I'll   take   my   chanc - es   I   for - got   how   nice   ro - mance   is

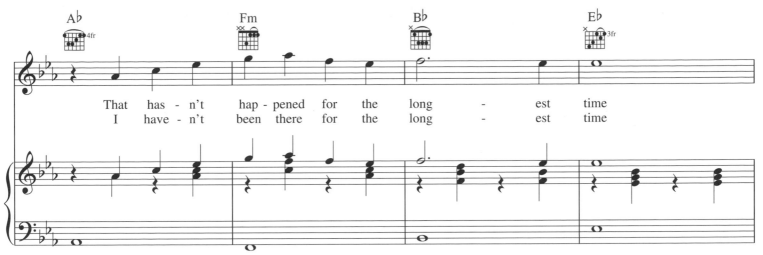

That has - n't hap - pened for the long - est time
I have - n't been there for the long - est time

May - be this won't last ver - y long But I
I had sec - ond thoughts at the long start

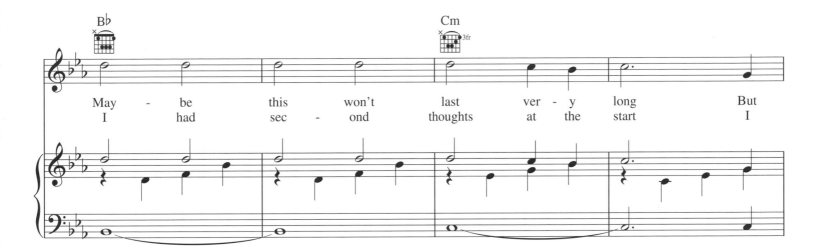

you feel so right And I could be wrong
said to my - self Hold on to your heart

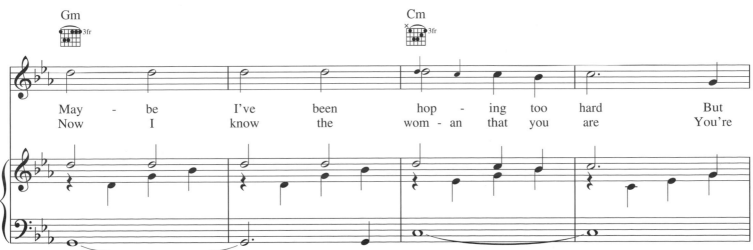

May - be I've been hop - ing too hard But
Now I know the wom - an that you are You're

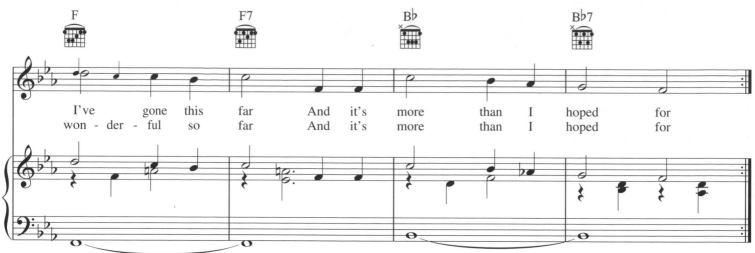

I've gone this far   And it's more than I hoped for
won-der-ful so far   And it's more than I hoped for

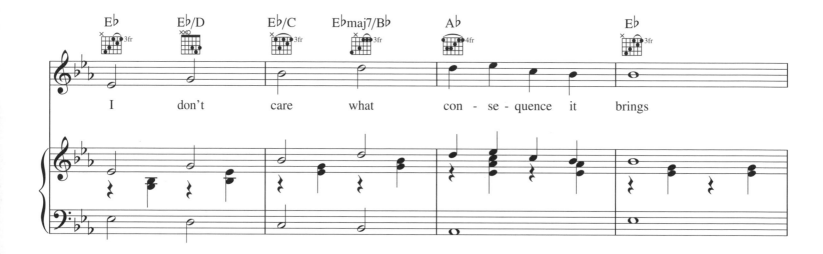

I don't care what con-se-quence it brings

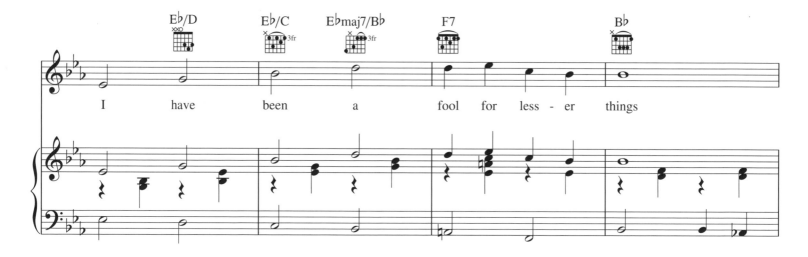

I have been a fool for less-er things

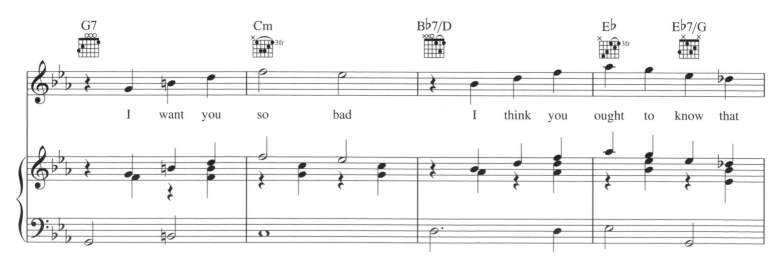

I want you so bad I think you ought to know that

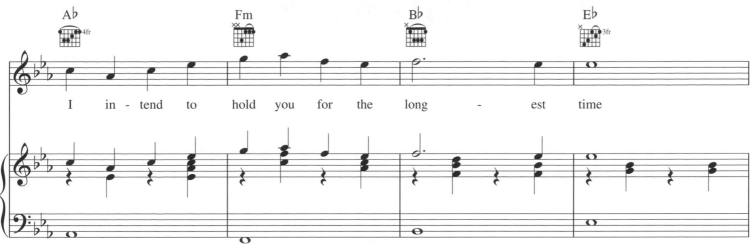

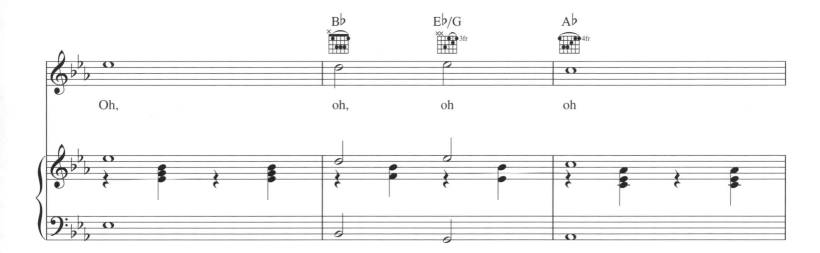

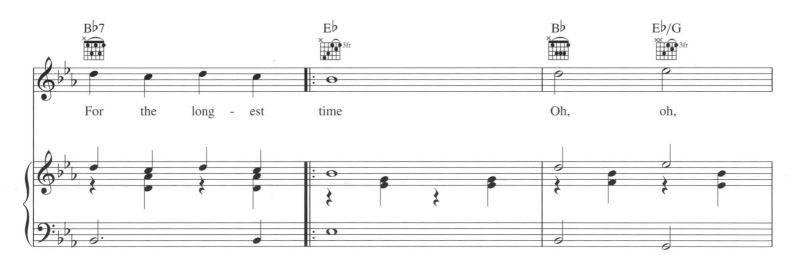

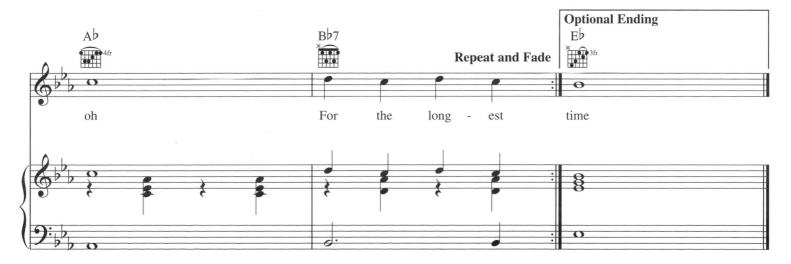

LULLABYE
(Goodnight, My Angel)

Words and Music by
BILLY JOEL

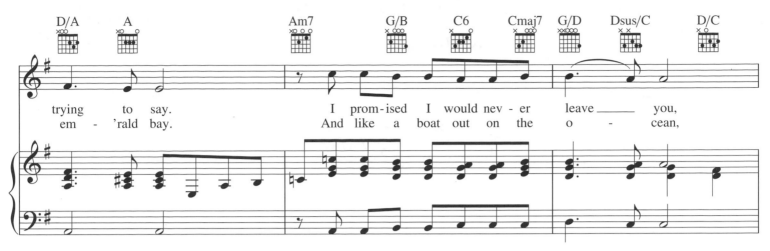

trying to say.
em - 'rald bay.
I prom-ised I would nev - er leave _____ you,
And like a boat out on the o - cean,

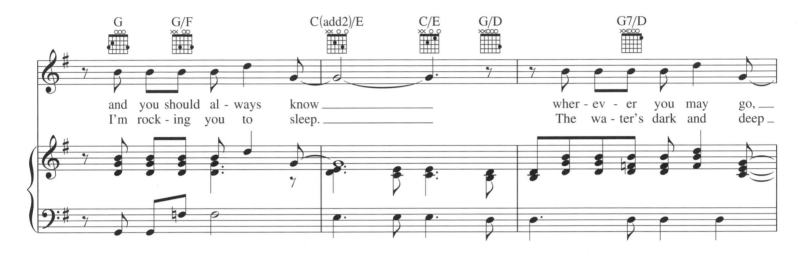

and you should al - ways know _____
I'm rock-ing you to sleep. _____
wher - ev - er you may go, _____
The wa - ter's dark and deep _____

_____ no mat - ter where you are, _____ I nev - er will be far a - way.
_____ in - side this an - cient heart _____ you'll al - ways be a

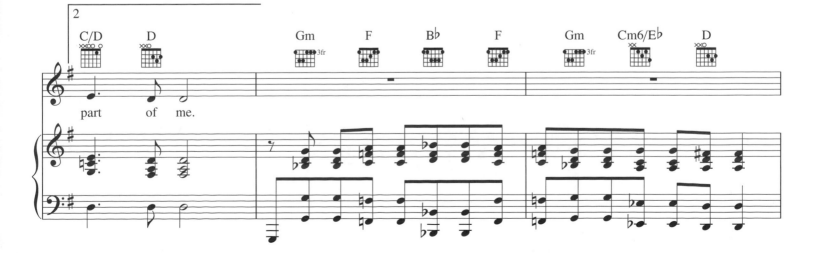

part of me.

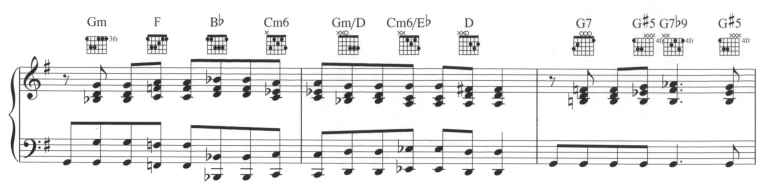

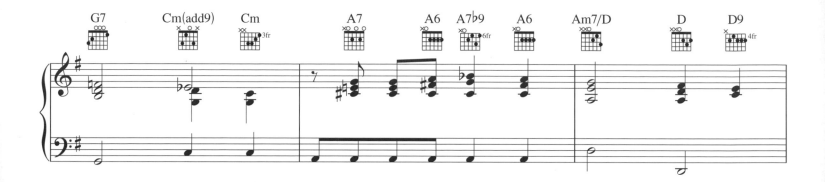

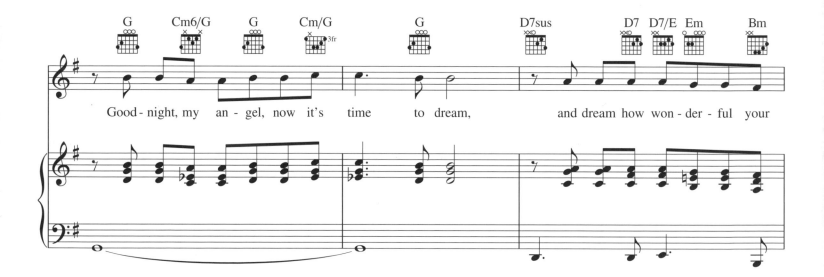

Good - night, my an - gel, now it's time to dream, and dream how won - der - ful your

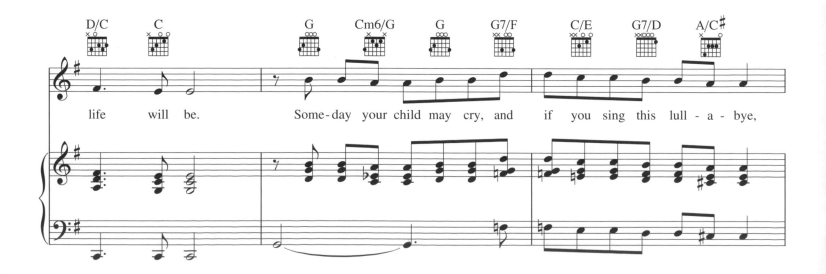

life will be. Some - day your child may cry, and if you sing this lull - a - bye,

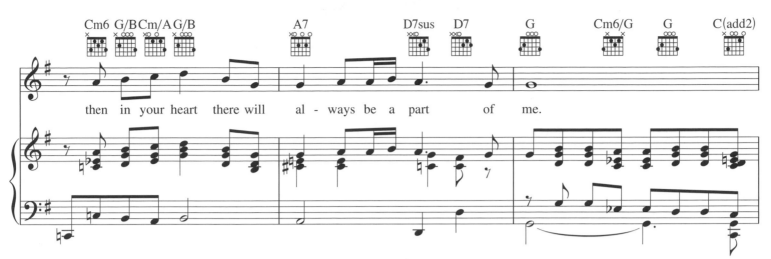

then in your heart there will al - ways be a part of me.

Some-day we'll all be gone but

lull - a - byes go on and on. They nev - er die, that's how you and _ I will

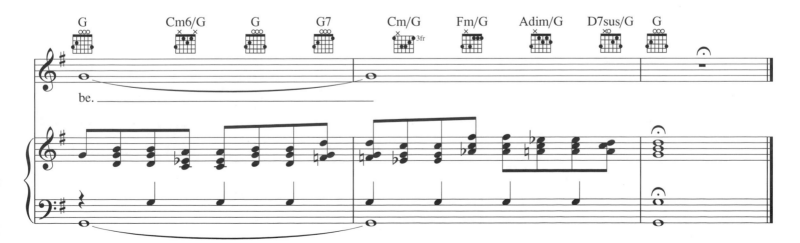

be. _____

MY LIFE

Words and Music by
BILLY JOEL

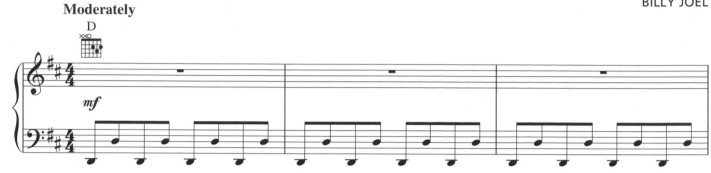

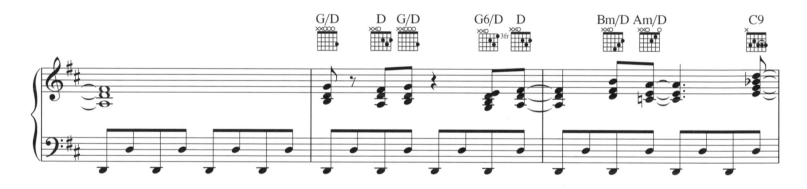

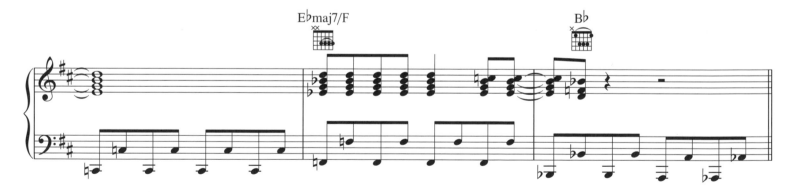

Play 1st time only *Play 2nd, 3rd and 4th times only*

D/F# Em D   A

Now he gives_ them a stand -
Go a - head_ with your own_
Ei - ther way,_ it's o - kay,_

1, 3
D   Bm/D Am/D   C9

- up rou - tine_ in L. A. _____
_____ life, __ leave _ me a - lone. __
_____ you wake up __ with your - self. _____

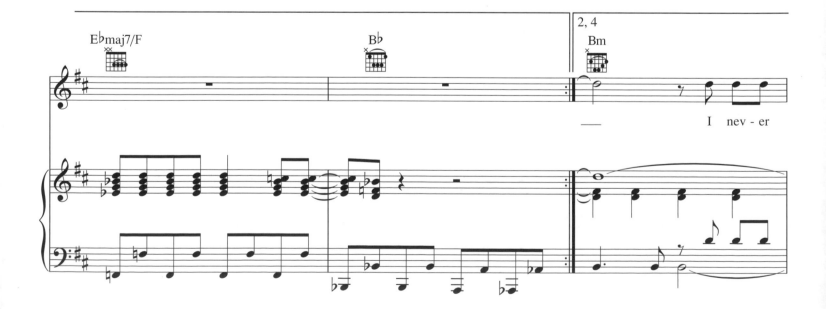

E♭maj7/F   B♭   2, 4
Bm

___ I nev - er

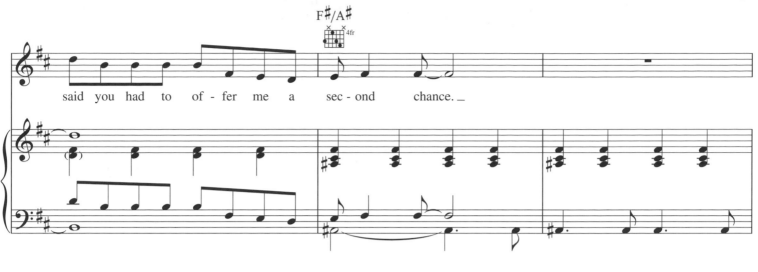

said you had to of-fer me a sec-ond chance. _

I nev-er said I was a vic-tim of cir - cum-stance. _____

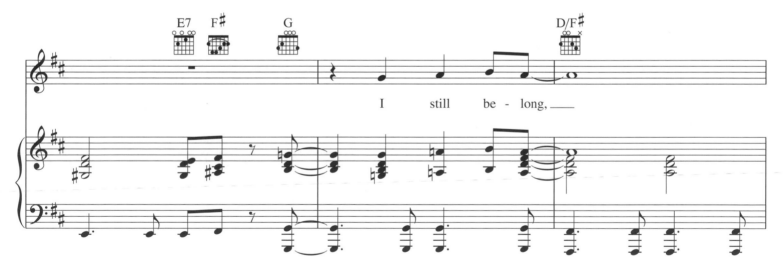

I still be-long, _____

don't get me wrong. _____ You _____ can speak _

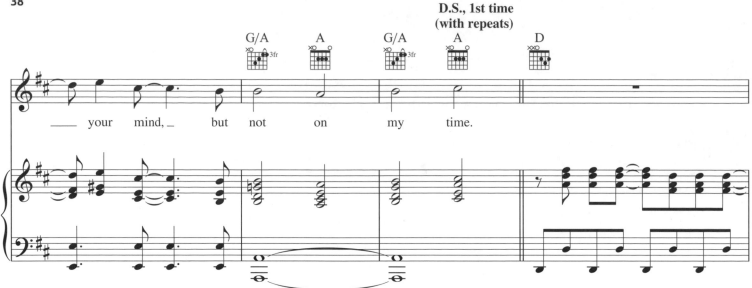

your mind, _ but not on my time.

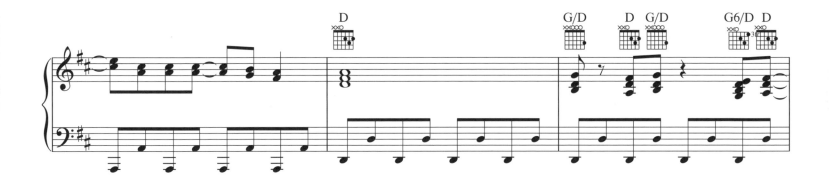

I don't care _ what you say _ an-y-more, _ this is my life.

Go a-head__ with your own__ life, leave me a-lone.__

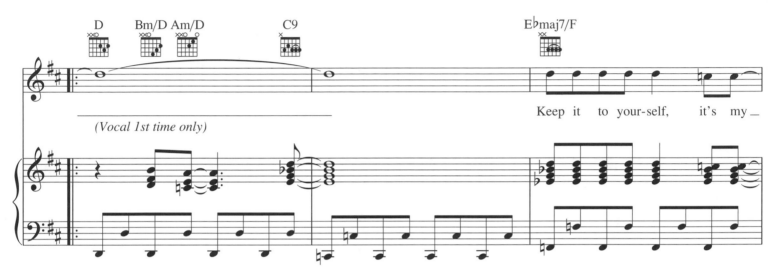

(Vocal 1st time only)

Keep it to your-self, it's my__

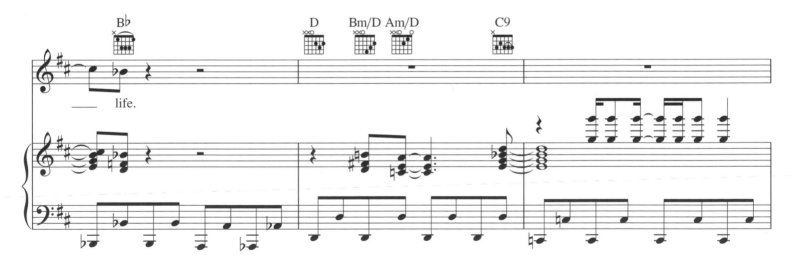

__ life.

Repeat and Fade

Optional Ending

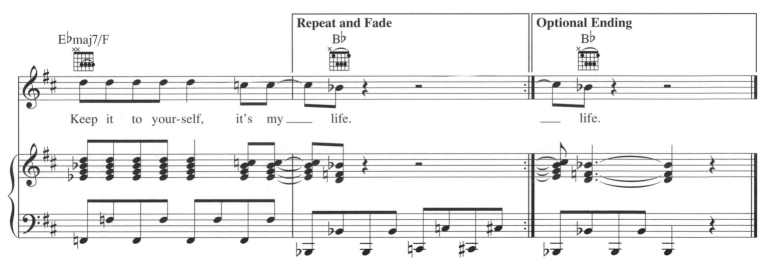

Keep it to your-self, it's my___ life.   ___ life.

NEW YORK STATE OF MIND

Words and Music by
BILLY JOEL

Slowly, with a Blues feel

(1.) Some folks __ like to get a - way take a
(2.) I've seen __ all the mov - ie stars in their
(3.,5.) Comes down __ to re - al - i - ty and it's
(4.) *Instrumental*

hol - i - day from the neigh - bor - hood, hop a flight to Mi -
fan - cy cars and their lim - ou - sines, been high in the
fine with me, 'cause I've let it slide. Don't care if it's

am - i Beach or to Hol - ly - wood.
Rock - ies __ un - der the ev - er - greens.
Chi - na - town or on Riv - er - side.

(1.,5., D.S.S.) But I'm tak - in' a Grey - hound on the Hud - son Riv - er line. __
But I know __ what I'm need - in' and I don't want to waste more
I don't have an - y rea - sons, I've left them all be -

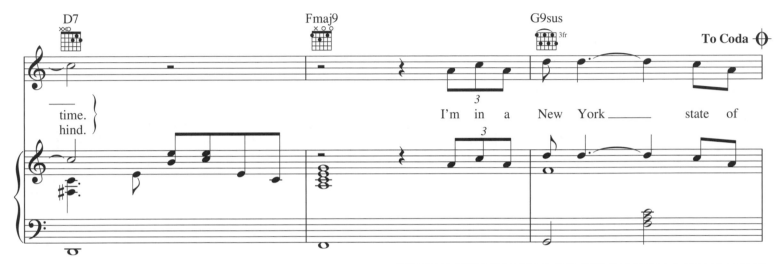

__ time.
__ hind.

I'm in a New York __ state of

To Coda ⊕

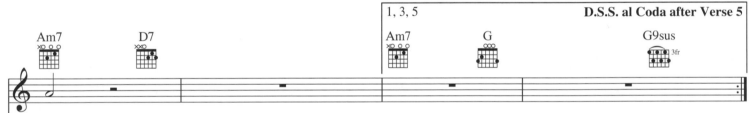

1, 3, 5

D.S.S. al Coda after Verse 5

mind.

2, 4

(2.,4.) It was so

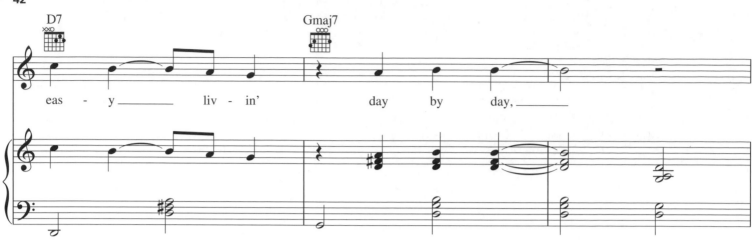

eas - y _____ liv - in' day by day, _____

out of touch with the rhy - thm and blues.

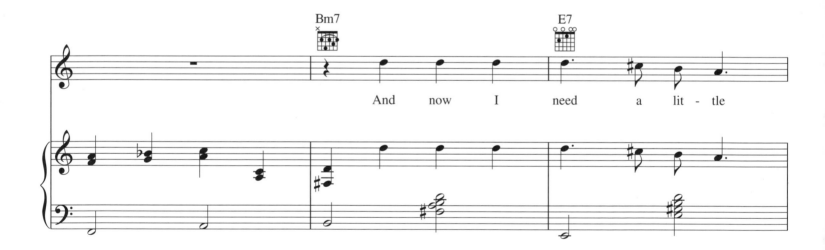

And now I need a lit - tle

give and take _____ the New York Times _____

the Dai - ly News.

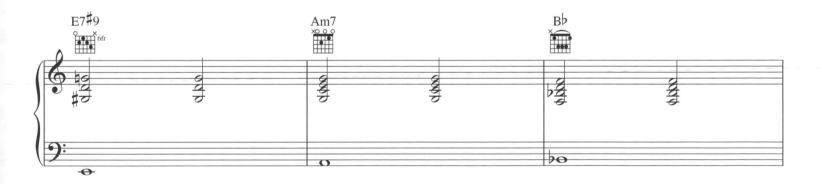

mind.

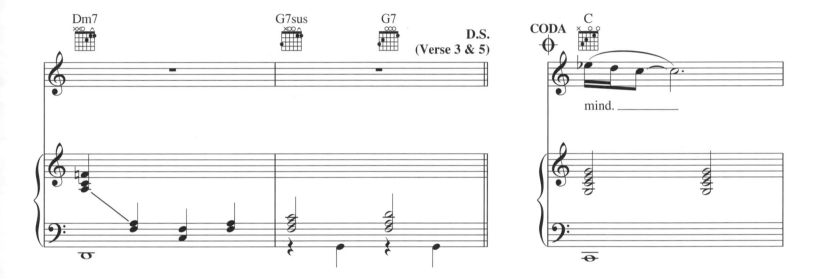

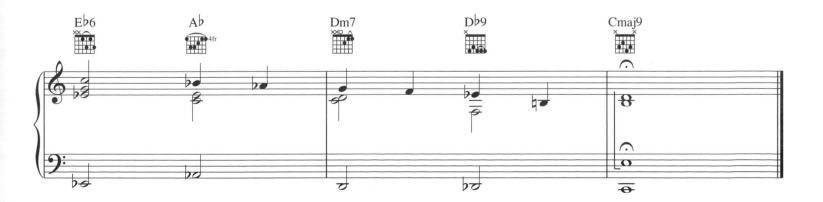

SHE'S GOT A WAY

Words and Music by
BILLY JOEL

Slow and steady

She's got a way ___ a-bout ___
She's got a smile ___ that heals ___

___ her. I don't know ___ what it is, ___ but I
___ me. I don't know ___ why it is, ___ but I

know that I ___ can't live with-out ___ her. She's got a way ___ of
have to laugh ___ when she re-veals ___ me. She's got a way ___ of

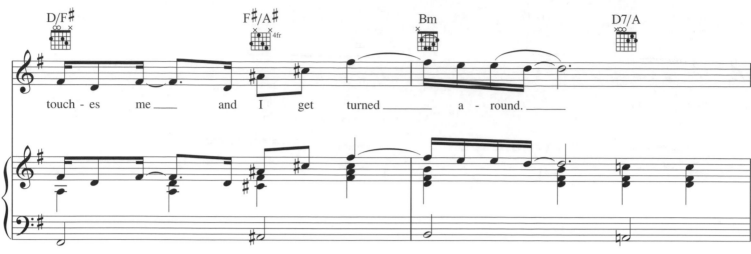

touch-es me ___ and I get turned ___ a - round. ___

She's got a way ___ of show - in'

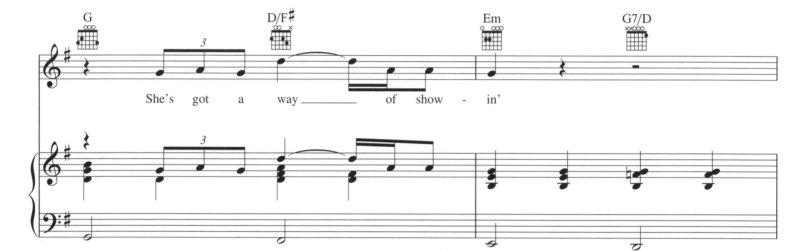

how I make her feel, ___ and I find the strength __ to keep __ on go - in'.

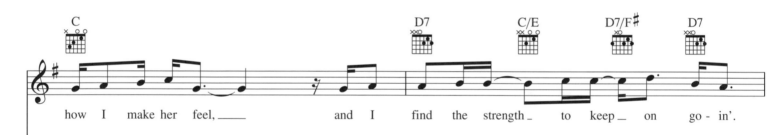

She's got a light ___ a - round her, and

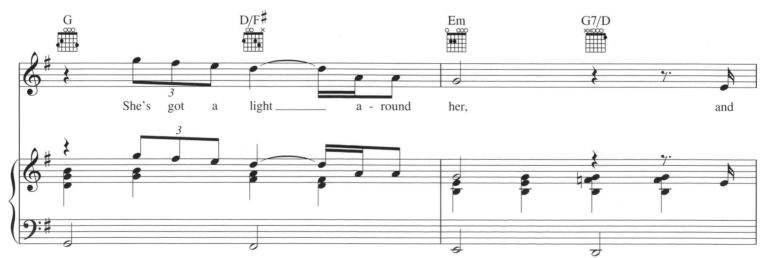

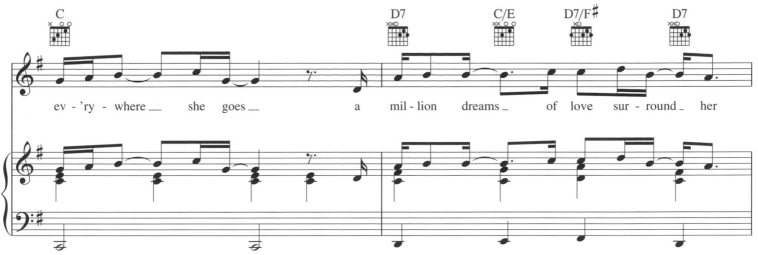

ev - 'ry - where __ she goes __ a mil - lion dreams __ of love sur - round __ her

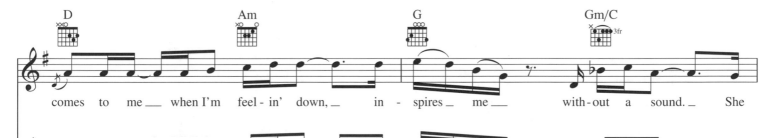

ev - 'ry - where. She

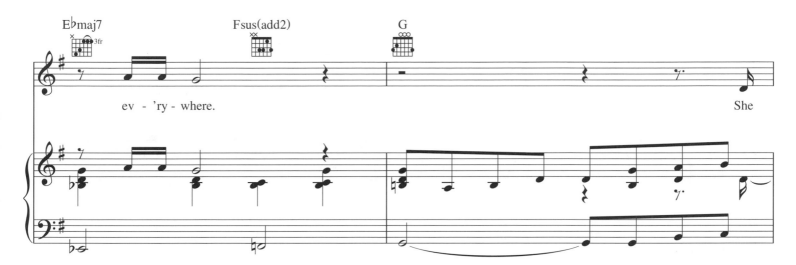

comes to me __ when I'm feel - in' down, __ in - spires __ me __ with - out a sound. __ She

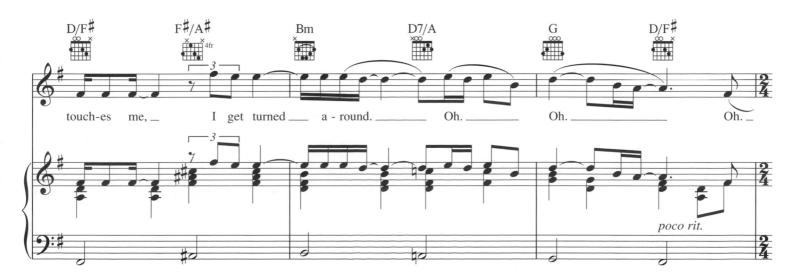

touch - es me, __ I get turned __ a - round. __ Oh. __ Oh. __ Oh. __

She's got a smile ___ that heals me. ___ I

don't know why it is, but I have to laugh ___ when she re-veals ___ me.

She's got a way ___ a-bout ___ her. I don't know ___ what it is, ___ but I

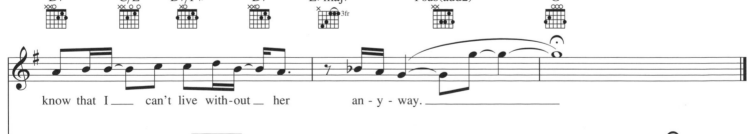

know that I ___ can't live with-out ___ her an-y-way. ___